MW01273167

Poems
of a
Different Kind

Dedication:

Thank you to all the wondrously talented Artists and Writers I drew Inspiration from.

The poems in
'Poems of a
Different Kind'
from chapters 1 - 5 are the
original work of Wayne C.
Hannis

www.waynehannis.ca

Table of Contents

Chapters

"A Writer must write!
No matter what
they may write!"

-said every Writer

Other Poets

1. Brett Harte (Francis) 1836 - 1902
   -What the Chimney Sang
2. William Butler Yeats 1865 - 1939
   -The Four Ages of Man
3. William Wordsworth 1770 - 1850
   -November 1836
4. Ella Wheeler Wilcox 1850 - 1919
   -The Worker and the Work
5. Henry Lawson 1867 - 1922
   -The Things We Dare not Tell
6. Yehuda Amichai 1924 - 2000
   -A Man doesn't have Time
7. Frances Ann Kemble 1809 - 1893
   -A Lament for the Wessahikon (Valley)
8. Robert Frost 1874 - 1963
   -The Road not Taken
9. Emily Pauline Johnson 1861 - 1913
   -Dawendine

www.darkpoets.club

I am to Die

Published by Dark Poets Club

On the skeleton of our need, why the horror of the leaving?
The folding up of the white narcissus, darker blue, the moon is white, the night an even hue.
These sounds of bones cracking back, the moans out of the night, crying, bitten.
I wonder what shapes they'll force, what tentacles they'll grow?
Pride swallowed, in the rich galled turnings of my throat.
Possess them in child magic, through all their dreary spread.
While I myself, edged into the terrible acute hatred.
I came to death, with my mind drowning.
The blood screaming, in the empty reservoir of bones.
Can they eat off my skeleton of pain, and die in the Aether Peripheries?
Now petal after petal, turns brown.
I move away in careless death, walking on long knives.

1. Fantasy

"Without this playing of Fantasy, no creative work has ever come to birth. The debt we owe to the play of the imagination is incalculable!"
-Carl Jung

A Dragon comes forth

A Dragon comes forth from her lair and
surveys the land below.
She has slept for an age in her deep cave
under the mountain.
She has awoken- not only because of
hunger- but for a need beyond her
understanding.

She may be the last dragon to remain in the
world,
she feels it deep inside.
A sorrow so profound
and a loneliness that consumes.

She stretches her wings, and on four legs she
bounds into the sky.
Hope will keep her aloft, as she begins her
search for others of her kind.

Her leathery wings take her far and wide,
she saw no other of her kind.
She sailed out to Sea,
but saw no Sea Dragon.
She climbed to the peaks of Mountains, she
found no life.
She went to the North,
no Snow Dragons were there.
She travelled to the Desert,
it too was dead.
She flew to the east,
but determined no Spirit.
She found no sign of
another Dragon.

She wondered what could have happened to
them?
Did they leave? Were they dead?
Or just hiding deep underground?
Was she truly the last of her kind?

She decided to go where
her wings couldn't carry her.
She followed wide passages
into the depths of the Earth.
The deeper she went
the hotter it became.
Until her four legs brought her
to her destination.

There she found
not another Dragon,
but instead three eggs
waiting to be cared for.
She wasn't the last of her kind after all .

Goblin in my head

Now I lay me down to sleep, and I pray to have
sweet dream.
But there's a Goblin sitting on my chest, and he
wants me to have nightmares.
Gross and disgusting, he sits and smiles his black
tooth grin.
In my mind I hear him say, "You will die!"
With visions of blood and gore he plays over and
over in my head- he torments me.
It's driving me insane.
Is he real or some figment of my imagination?
Is it me or is it him- that bring these thoughts to
my mind?
Will I live or will I die, or will the agony be
prolonged?
The Goblin sitting on my chest embraces me,
holding me tight.
Suddenly I realize- the Goblin is me!

Humpty Dumpty

There was once an egg- a fairly large one, for an egg that is. He was short and stout and wore a pair of overalls cut off at the knees. His name was Humpty Dumpty. It was a fitting name, for he wasn't too bright and he was rather round, for an egg that is.

Humpty lived in a time when kings and queens ruled the land and everything was made from stone and brick. As you can guess, this wasn't the safest place for an egg the live. But Humpty never thought of the dangers, living his life in peaceful bliss, for he was just an egg.

One day, with the sun shinning in the sky, Humpty Dumpty was sitting on a wall. Not being very intelligent that day, for he was just an egg, he was swaying his legs back and forth. He swung his legs to high and toppled over backwards. Humpty Dumpty had a great fall.

When he landed his shell shattered, splattering his insides all over the sidewalk. Humpty cried in pain, screaming for all the kings horses and all the kings men to, "Please, put me together again." When they arrived- trying to no avail, couldn't put Humpty Dumpty together again.

Humpty Dumpty died soon after, and the whole city mourned his passing because he was a lovable egg. At his wake, the people followed through with his last wish. They scrambled him up and had a great feast. They would all remember Humpty Dumpty with fond memories.

"Fantasy is hardly an escape from reality. It's a way of understanding it.
-Lloyd Alexander
1924-2007

"Fantasy is a
necessary ingredient
in living!"
-Theodor Seuss Geisel
1904-1991

"We live in a Fantasy World, a world of illusion. The great task in life is to find reality."
-Iris Murdoch
1919-1999

"If one is lucky, a solitary fantasy can totally transform one million realities."
-Mya Angelou
1928-2014

2. Lamentations

"Sometimes you laugh because you've got
no more room for crying."
-Terry Pratchett
1948-2015

"Every Person has his secret sorrow which
the world knows not, and often times we
call a person cold when they are only sad."
-Henry Wadsworth Longfellow
1807-1882

"The perfected future never arrives. Life is
full of seemingly endless trouble, and then
you die. Find peace in the imperfect."
-Marcus Aurelius: The Stoic Emperor
121-180

"But now- now, when a lull in the storm gave brief respite from the fury of the wind- now a man might let himself mourn at last, and lay the ghosts to rest."
-Kathern Kurtz: American Fantasy Author
"Joy, sorrow, tears, lamentation, laughter- to all these music gives voice, but in such a way that we are transported from the world of unrest to a world of peace, and see reality in a new way, as if we were sitting by a mountain lake and contemplating hills and woods and clouds in the tranquil and fathomless water."
-Albert Schweitzer
1875 - 1965

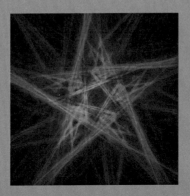

A Lament for Meka

1.

There was a Man who had a dog.
She was the most beautiful and faithful
companion that could ever be,
and He loved Her dearly.

They spent every day together.
The Man never left Her behind,
And She was always eager to go.

They took long walks together.
Up mountain trails they roamed,
While She, off-leash, was never out of sight.

Downtown to the city streets they went,
He was always proud walking beside Her.
She would greet everyone they encountered
with kindness and a smile.

2.

For years they were together, through all the
trials and tribulations of life.
At night She would sleep next to Him,
and during the day She was always by His
side.
She was his life.

But in the short life of a dog,
She quickly grew old.
Before the Man knew, She drew close to
death.

He made Her as comfortable as He could, as
they waited for the end.
He watched hopelessly,
as She slowly slipped away,
And on a Thursday, late afternoon,
She died naturally.
His Soul Mate was gone.

3.

The Man grieved deeply
for His lost companion,
The tears would not cease.
His days changed drastically,
She was no longer by His side.
His life would never be the same.

He missed Her so much.
His heart was broken beyond repair,
For the loss of his Beautiful and Faithful
Companion.

Life went on and the Man never forgot,
Those long walks with his
beautiful dog,
And longed for those days.

In the fullness of time,
the Man eventually died as well.
Glad He was when Death
finally came for Him,
He hoped, after all the years apart,
He would see His Soul Mate again.
He had never let Her go.

4.
He awoke suddenly in a field of grass,
with blue and white flowers
all around.
In the distance He saw a forest full of spruce
and fir- just like back home.

He surmised He was in
The Elysian fields,
perhaps Nirvana or Shangri-la.
He new not which, as He looked around in
anticipation to see his Faithful Companion.

He looked down, and there She was,
His Soul Mate was by His side.
She looked up to Him
with Her familiar big brown eyes,
and a smile on Her face.
She was young again

5.

She was like when they took long walks up
forest trails and on the downtown streets.
Both man and dog were different inside,
Not what they once were on the Earth below.

Her sleek black coat glimmered in the glorious
golden sun,
All Her grey was gone.
And He stood tall without aches or pains.

Their love for each other flourished
once again,
As they walked on the path
through the field.
She was always within his sight.

They had no destination,
it did not matter.
They were together again.

6.

Eventually they came to a golden gate, shining
opalescent in the distant sun.
The gate was closed,
baring any entrance.
A brick wall stretched into infinity
on either side.

White puffy clouds were all around,
with people lounging in luxury.
"This must be Heaven,"
the man said to His dog.
"The Kingdom of the Most High."

The Gate Keeper came out,
and stood at the gate.
"Can we come in?" the man asked.
"Yes- you can," the Gate Keeper replied.
"But not your dog. An unclean animal can not
enter into paradise."

7.
The man did not hesitate.
"Forget it then," he stated.
"I would rather spend eternity in Hades with
her, than in Heaven without her.
I have already been through Hell without Her,
all those years on Earth.
She is my Soul Mate- I'll never leave Her
behind."

The Man and his dog quickly turned,
Leaving the Gates to
The Celestial Kingdom behind.
They never looked back,
As they headed down the trail.

The Gate Keeper watched them leave
perplexed.
But man and his dog he did not see- instead- a
man and another.
A woman, with long, dark hair glistening in the
golden sun, beside Him.
They walked into Eternity together.

In Memory of

Meka Hannis

my beautiful and faithfull
dog.

She was 17 years old.

Born early spring 2004
Died Thursday
late afternoon
April 8, 2021.
Naturally!

Retreat within my Thoughts

Retreat within my thoughts, the visions that I
imagine.
Darkness behind, and the things before me,
are they tangible? are they real?
Or is it some kind of Hell created just for me?
Seeing such beauty and not be able to feel.
So far out of reach I cannot touch.
Wishing I could grasp on to something
to let me know I'm alive.
Inside my mind, the desires that I hold,
consumes from within.
I cannot let them out,
for the embers would set my soul on fire.
Hope is a fleeting thing,
It fools me when I do.
Alone I shall remain unable to hope,
For it will destroy me if I let it.

A Shattered Soul

I have always contemplated my own Mortality,
someday I will Die!
It seems there are more Days behind than
ahead.
Soon that Day will arrive, I know not when.
Humans have always endeavoured to do Good,
as we have the will to do Good.
But as Positive and Negative, so is the Human
Will to do Evil.
If the desire is to do Good, one must
continually strive to over come the Evil
Nature.
Diversity runs deep in the Human Soul,
some don't understand the Pain they may
cause.
They don't understand the Evil they do.
One Man grieves with the Pain he sees,
while another revels in the Madness of
Suffering.
We can't comprehend how Empathy can heal
a Shattered Soul,
when everything that is can be known.

My Hands are stained in Blood

I have been to war.
My hands are stained in blood.
Will the guilt ever leave?

I have killed so close, recognition would
have stopped me.
I have killed from so far,
they could have been anyone.
All of them had someone that loved them and
children to cherish.
They all had someone to look up to, someone
who taught them right from wrong.
Just like I did.
Taking a life is akin to extinguishing the sun,
no one should have the power.
My hands have felt the blood of those lives I
ended.
There families will never see them again.

But now my blood stains the hands of another.
Killed from afar so I could have been anyone.
If they were close, would I recognize them?
Say 'good bye' to those I love.

I have been to war.
My hands are stained in blood.
Will the guilt ever leave.

Words so Tender
Words so Soft

Words so tender
Words so soft
To give me wonderful thoughts
Words so tender
Words so soft
To fill my soul full of happiness and fill my life
full of wonderful thoughts
Words so tender
Words so soft
Is all I need to hear to fill my soul and give me
wonderful thoughts
When you speak words so tender and words so
soft
You fill my soul to give me wonderful thoughts
When I have wonderful thoughts to fill my
soul
I will speak to you in words so tender and
words so soft

Will You Remember?

For purposes unknown, two lives brought
together.
Fate's hand at work, in the weaving of the
tapestry.
You came to me when my life was down,
To spend awhile, then leave.
I came to you when you didn't know where
to turn,
To spend awhile, then leave.
Presently you are by my side,
but tomorrow I could be gone.
For something so fragile we still hold on,
and tomorrow you could be gone.
If you leave tomorrow,
I will still remember today.
One day Fate's hand will intervene and take
me away.
I would hope you will still remember me.

Ode to The Shuswap

Take me back to the
Mountains,
Where my Spirit soars so
high.

Only on mountain trails or
along rocky shores,
is my mind content.

Roaring springs of fresh
water rushing from the
rocky peaks,
to rejuvenate my soul.

Where spruce and fir
grow tall reaching for the
sky,
and their roots go deep
into the fertile earth.

In lush green valleys
with a creek flowing
nearby,
Is where I want to be.

Take me back to the
mountains,
where the Highlands
reflect my soul.

Adams River
   Canyon

"It is extremely dangerous to make sport of the Mysteries of Magic; it is above all excessively rash to practice its rites from curiosity, by way of experiment and as if to exploit higher forces. The inquisitive who, without being adepts, busy themselves with evocations or occult magnetism, are like children playing with fire in the neighbourhood of a cask of gun powder; sooner or later they will fall victims to such a terrible explosion."

-Elephaz Levis: 1810-1875
Transcendental Magic

3.Metaphysics
The Philosophical study of Being & Knowing

"I study myself more than any other subject.
That is my Metaphysics, that is my Physics."
-Michel de Montaigne
1533-1592

"A Morning Glory in my window satisfies me
more than the Metaphyisics of books"
-Walt Whitman
1819-1892

"To regard the imagination as Metaphysics is to
think of it as part of life, and to think of it as
part of life is to realize the extent of art. We live
in the mind."
-Wallace Stevens
1879-1955

"Though the modern world may know a million secrets, the ancient world knew one- and that was greater than the million, for the million secrets breed death, disaster, sorrow, selfishness, lust, and avarice, but the one secret confers life, light, and truth."
"They wander in darkness seeking light, failing to realize that the light is in the heart of the darkness."
-Manly P. Hall: 1901-1990

"I am the consciousness that controls the body of, sees through the eyes of, and hears the thoughts of this person.
-Terry Pratchett: 1949 - 2015

"In the Universe, there are things that are known and things that are unknown, and in between, are doors."
-William Blake: 1757 - 1827

Reach across the Aether

Musicians are Magicians using the
Magnetism of Sound and Vibration.
Harmony is the Essence of nature.

Electricity is the Aether in discharge,
demonstrating itself as Electricity.

In Golden Ratios the One manifests
the Absolute,
in the growth of all things.

We are all Energy Beings from the Aether,
and the only thing that is Infinite is the
Imagination.

As We reach across the Aether,
the Will to Live is stronger than the Will to
Die.

Memory is a Strange Thing

When I was young the remembrance of an
incident was sharp and clear,
Images I could see within my mind played over
and over again.

As I have aged, those things I once did seem
scattered and out of focus,
displaced within my thoughts.

I know when I get old it will be as if those
experiences that shaped who I am,
will be gone and lost forever. Forgotten in time.

But that is the fate of us all.

A Beautiful Thought

Look around- see the sunshine with the moon
in a clear blue sky.
See the clouds above- there's been a change
in the air,
and it's as if the sky is higher than it ever was
before.

Imagine a beautiful thought and have it
become real.
Feel the magic around us, but do not speak
only half a spell.
There may be dire consequences if you do.

In order to contain all the knowledge of the
Universe,
you would need a larger Universe to keep it in.

Our whole Paradigm is a facade,
it's time to peer beyond the Veil,
we must know what's beyond.

Trust only those who say they are seeking the
truth,
but never trust those who claim to know the
truth.

Life is a Mystery,
and everything is Theory.

Reality is Different

In times gone past and in times to come,
I sit here in the now watching and waiting.
I hope to see the past develop into the
future.

The Present tells the story of things still to
occur,
If you look real close the future may reveal
itself to you.
Based upon the past, the things that
happened will lead you.

Reality is different for each individual,
But remains a constant for all.
Where do I come from? Where do I go?
Above all else- What am I doing here?

My mental stability pounding away,
Forever questioning the very thought of life.
The fabric of my brain melting away,
To leave nothing but an empty inquiry.

Time flowing by- I can't hold on any more.
I see it will lead me into blackness where
nothing else matters,
Only the thought of once was.

Day after Day I continue,
Tomorrow will be the same as Yesterday.
Night after Night I sit here in the Now,
With this emptiness inside.

The Pain subsides one day,
The next it comes double fold.
The question no longer remains,
So I will never find the answer.

Walking the Road of Death,
Lost Souls wonder aimlessly,
The trail is as black as night.

The first step is the easiest as you place your
foot on the ever winding path.
Stumble and fall, and it will be your last.

Even though the Road to Hell is paved with
good intentions,
The Ruler of Darkness awaits.

As I dream of what tomorrow may bring,
In the morning I will know the fear of the
day before.
Only in the memory of my minds eye does
the past exist,
And the future solely a dream.

In the Now

In times gone past
and in times to come;
I sit here in the now,
watching and waiting,
waiting and watching.
For the past to envelop into the future.

The present tells the story of things to
come.
In the now you may see,
if you look real close,
The future may reveal itself to you.

Reality is different for each individual,
But for all it remains a constant.

Only in the memory of my minds eye does
the past exist,
And the future only a dream.

The Sea of Oblivion

As time moves on,
death will come to all.

Countless people that once lived,
now cast adrift in 'The Sea of Oblivion'.
They were remembered only for a while.

Kings and World Movers are the only ones
remembered forever.
But only as names written within a book.

All the lives ever lived, now forgotten within
'The Sea of Oblivion'.

You and I shall also be cast adrift in
'The Sea of Oblivion',
to be remembered only for a while.

The memory of us shall fade and be forgotten.
As we are cast adrift in
'The Sea of Oblivion'.

Absolutes in a World of Grey

The light of a Moral Law illuminates the
differences between good and evil,
and distinguishes between right and wrong.
Distinctly defining day from night,
light and darkness.

Governed by moral duties it invokes a moral
sense within a person,
to perceive the capacity for benevolence
and malice.

According to their conscience they judge,
between the two- right or wrong.

They apply this philosophy of the nature and
grounds,
of moral obligation to their own life,
whether for good or for evil.

The immoral person removes themselves
from this strict law of absolutes.
They are unable to perceive the capacity for
benevolence and malice.
They are wicked and inequitable- having no
conscience,
to judge between good and evil.
Blurring the intangible law they create
shades of grey,
Where there was once only light and dark.
Being inconsistent and contrary to morality,
They undermine and corrupt the morals of
other,
Rendering them distrustful and hopeless.
In such a world- a good man becomes rich,
and an evil man goes to church.

-Definitions for Morality and Immorality
were taken from:
'The New Webster Encyclopedic Dictionary
of the English Language' 1978.

The Way I See it

A Shadow is gathering,
and deep darkness is amassing.

A storm is coming,
and soon we shall all be hidden from the light.

Fleeting hope is all we have to survive,
and a spark within the mind.

The magic has been woven
and the battle must be won.

Things are twisted,
and only a few have awaken.

Its one step away,
and the world is waiting in ignorance.

The noose around our necks is being pulled tighter,
as the subjection within our minds become real.

Strange things are happening all around,
are they real or illusion?

The Veil between Worlds is weakening-
Whats on the other side?

Our children are being taught by those who create
weapons of mass destruction.
Bring them to corrupted morals.
And all we say is: "Lets go take that ride."
Will they escape the war that is coming?

Governments of nations fabricate
a countenance of peace,
Meanwhile behind closed doors
they plan for genocide.
Poisoning us in the air, food and water,
In order to reduce the human population.

We are continuously being told the lie,
"We are responsible!
for the death of the world."
And in truth our Mother Earth can abundantly
supply for all of her children's needs.
All we need to do is live in peace.

The spell of money keeps us enslaved,
Bringing us all deeper into debt.
Soon the bubble will explode,
to leave us with nothing.
It's all an illusion anyway,
something that doesn't truly exist.

Earthquakes shaking deep underground.
Mountains ejecting molten rock
and thick gray clouds,
Blanketing continents and bringing them to a
deadlock,
With rumors of it all being created by man.

Were we created by an omnipotent being in His
image?
Or was our DNA constructed by a race from the
distant reaches of our galaxy?
The answer to those question and more are still open
to interpretation.
As we are manipulated by
generational mind control.

There still is a glimmer of hope
within the darkness.
We must love instead of hate,
as many have taught.
And through peace we must react.

In this way only, we will see the truth and bring about
a New World Order for the benefit of all.

The way I see it anyway.

Metaphysics of Architecture

1.

Architecture speaks to us down through the ages- Sacred Geometry shaped in brick and stone is the written language, 'The Universal Communication'.

Architecture is the only Art
by which we can understand Nature,
as Nature is Architecture.

Architecture through Sacred Geometry
is a means by which the Divine speaks to us.

Philosophers recreate the Infinity, multiplied without end, with no fixed boundary- which makes objects seem to extend forever, and the Imagination have no rest.

Just as with Nature
we only see a continuation without beginning,
and without end.
It becomes the power to effect what only
Poetry can described.

2.

Through the effects of Light Architecture has
the capacity of stirring the Soul to make us
experience the horrors of Darkness,
or bring us through the sublime,
as to create Light within our Spirit.

It is a historical exchange
between the real and the ideal-
by the manipulation of Light
it invokes a response within human emotions.

The geometric shapes render Architecture
transcendent- in which darkness, and the
pyramidal form,
with domed roofs and columns one after
another, evoke the end of life.

We climb stairs that assend into Darkness, and
emerge into the Sacred Space, where the
Architect recreates light at the centre of the
Universe, and we see our precarious
metaphysical place within that universe.

3.

Within a sphere- at the very centre of brick, stone and glass- we can envision the entire Realm of our existence from the inside only.

Architecture and Geometry collide and coalesce to work as one to create the image of transcendence.

We are enlightened through Architecture, as it creates and transcends Infinity- while the Architect struggles to re-imagine the Heavens.

"Time is a Storm in which we are all lost."
-William Carlos Williams
1883-1963

"How did it get so late so soon? It's night before it's afternoon. December is here before it's June. My goodness how the time has flown. How did it get so late so soon?
-Theodor Seuss Geisel (Dr. Seuss)
1904-1991

"Time brings all things
to pass."
-Aeschylus
525-456B.C.E

4. Religion

"Trust those who say they are seeking the truth. Never trust those who claim to know the truth. Life is a mystery and everything is Theory."

"The Modern age is characterized by a sadness that calls for a new kind of Prophet, not like the Prophets of old who reminded the people that they were going to die, but someone who would remind them they are not dead yet."
-GK Chesterton
1834 - 1936

"Only those who step lightly in the world have a chance of being free from it for all time."
-Ken Wheeler: Metaphysician

"Many good sayings are to be found in Holy Books, but merely reading them will not make one religious"
-Ramakrishna
1836 - 1886

"Religion is everywhere. There are no human societies without it, whether they acknowledge it as religion or not."
-Octavia Butler
1947 - 2006

"Heaven is under our feet as well as over our heads."
-Henry David Thoreau
1817 - 1862

"Religion is what keeps the Poor from murdering the Rich."
Napoleon Bonaparte
1769 - 1821

He is God in Heaven

He is God in heaven above and on the earth below.
God of all the kingdoms of the earth.

God of Abraham, Isaac. and Jacob.
He is God of all living
and God of all the spirits of all flesh.

God of glory and God of mercy and peace.
He is the Living and True God, who along is wise;
the Faithful One.

The Everlasting Great and Awesome God.
He is Jesus, our Great God and Savior.

He is the image of the invisible God,
The One who built all things.

He forms the mountains and creates the wind.
He calls for the waters of the sea.

He makes the morning darkness,
And the day dark as night.

He also turns the shadow of death into dawn,
And is the only hope in the day of gloom:
a refuge from the storm.

He is the True Bread from heaven,
the Bread of Life;
And the Breath of the Almighty.

He is the Fountain of Living Water;
And the True and Everlasting Light of Life.

He is Jesus, the Great and Everlasting King
over all the earth;
And King of Heaven.

He is abounding in goodness and truth;
Acquainted with grief.

He searches the mind and heart, revealing His secrets;
And declares to man what His thoughts are.

He is the Commander of Yahweh's army,
The One who comes in the Name of Yahweh.
The Desire of all Nations.

The One who is and who was and who is to come,
He was dead and came to life and who lives.
The Heir of all things.

He is Jesus, the Author and Finisher of our faith;
The Author of Eternal Salvation.

He is the Resurrection and the Life.
The Savior of the World, The Way, The Truth and the Life.
Our Redeemer from Everlasting.

He loves us and washed us from our sin.
The Lamb without blemish and without spot.
The Lamb of God, who was slain.

He is our righteousness and sanctification and redemption.

He is Jesus, Son of David; The Lion of the tribe of Judah.
And He stands ready to judge the living and the dead.

-All references to Jesus are from the Bible
    -Translations were not taken into account

A Prayer to the Celtic gods

'The Mighty Three'
My protection be
Encircle me
You are around my home
You are around my Life
Encircle me, 'O Sacred Three'
'The Mighty Three'
I ask the 'Maker of the Sky'
of the 'Earth'
of the 'Water'
To encircle me
May You surround me with your love
To protect me today and every day
As I stand in the World

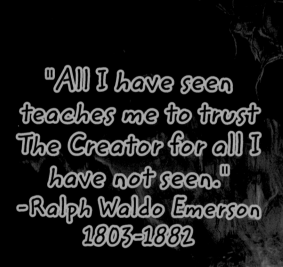

"All I have seen
teaches me to trust
The Creator for all I
have not seen."
-Ralph Waldo Emerson
1803-1882

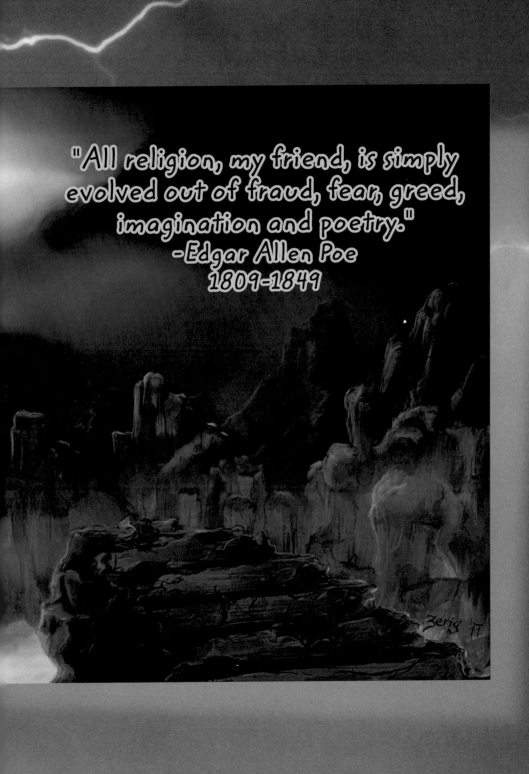

5. Excerpts from 'Dark Tales of Fantasy'

* * * * * *

When Evil Things happen to Good People, there never is a happy ending.

Dark Tales of Fantasy

When Evil Things happen to Good People, there never is a happy ending.

Five stories (novellas) of classical fantasy with a touch of horror from debut author Wayne C. Hannis.

Myth and magic collide in these tales of tragedy, when Evil Things happen to Good People.

Like Oril Ahern, Regent of the Kingdom of Tasmorea. All he wants is to hand the throne to his nephew. Prince Coel Ahern, heir to the Northern Throne, believes it is his "To Rule by Right" now that he has come of age.

And Niall Emayn, a black smith who just wants to live his life with his family, until a stranger appears and hires him to forge a sword. Niall will soon learn how "The Sword cuts deep". Because in the end, when Evil Things happen to Good People, there never is a happy ending.

Including: To Rule by Right
True Love Lost Forever -
A Man Caught in Time
The Sword Cuts Deep
A Contract for Gold- The
Cataclysm of Medhebah

Hobgoblins

Hobgoblins are nasty creatures
with vile intent.
They raid and pillage
just to see the blood.
Slaughtering whole families
is what makes them happy.
Just to hear the screams
excites them.

Hobgoblins are loathsome brutes
with a deceiving smile.
You will know if you ever meet one.
The last thing you will see
is the Hobgoblin laughing,
as he cuts off your head
with his rusted weapon.
It makes him euphoric just to watch you die,
and see you writhe in pain.

So don't go out of your way
to make a Hobgoblin felicitous.
Because he will surely
revel in your blood.

Hobgoblins find their own merriment
it's not hard for them to do.

If you ever encounter one of the despicable
creatures you will know,
as he's dancing on your corpse.

-Handbook of the Goblinkind, pg 27
-Carfaren Wynrel: Bard of Magical Secrets of
the College of Lore.

From 'Dark Tales of Fantasy: To Rule by Right'

We will all dwell in the grave

"A Rich Man rejoices,
while a Poor Man greives.
We will all dwell in the grave.

But when a Rich Man grieves,
a Poor Man will rejoice.
We will all dwell in the grave."

Thalia Hephekah

Dark Tales of Fantasy
A Contract for Gold:
The Cataclysm of Medhebah

The Banshee

On a long and lonely night,
you will hear her mournful wails.
In the Darkness,
She sings her Song of Death.
She died long ago,
no one now remembers how.
She laments over her loss,
and the suffering She endured.
The Wind conveys her doleful Dirge,
as you here it in your mind-
She's calling you to your destruction.
You will feel Her grief,
and in empathy you will listen to Her summons.
You cannot deny a Dead One's cry.

-Encyclopedia of the Dead, pg 531
-Dark Tales of Fantasy:
True Love Lost Forever

Darkness is the Absolute

Before Light existed,
darkness was already sempiternal.
In the absence of Light there is Darkness,
but in the absence of Darkness,
there is only more intense Darkness.

There are different depths to Darkness,
just as there are many degrees of Light,
and Darkness separates them all.

In the abyss of Darkness,
there contains infinite passages
forever cast in Shadow,
that lead to darker Shadows still.
Unimaginable Horrors dwell there.

All things come from the Darkness,
and all things are created in the Darkness,
including Light.
-The Deleth Ruwach Grimoire
-'Dark Tales of Fantasy:
True Love Lost Forever

A Man I Cannot See

This morning I saw a man I cannot see,
Out of the corner of my eye- he was there!
Standing, watching me.
But as I turned to see- he was not there!

This afternoon I saw a man I cannot see.
Out of the corner of my eye- he was there!
I think he's following me.
But as I turned to see- he was not there!

This evening I saw a man I cannot see,
Out of the corner of my eye- he was there!
I think he means me harm.
But as I turned to see- he was not there!

Tonight I saw a man I cannot see,
Out of the corner of my eye- he was there!
I think he intends to end my life.
But as I turned to see- he was not there!

Oh, how I wish this man I cannot see,
Would go away!
But as I turned to see- he was there!

-Experiences with Shadows, pg 72
Balashi Hunzuu, Sorcerer of Wild-Magic
-'Dark Tales of Fantasy: A Man Caught in Time'

A Door through the Veil

One Soul will grieve
with the pain they see.
While another delights
in the madness of suffering.

Within each mind is contained
the nature of good and evil,
the consciousness is a river
that runs deep.

As Blood brings forth life,
so the shedding of blood
brings forth death.

Blood will open the door through the veil
where time has no meaning.

-Written somewhere within
'The Ancient Book of Secrets'
-Author unknown
-'Dark Tales of Fantasy: The Sword Cuts
Deep'

The City that Fell

In the City that climbed so high, yet fell so low,
they wanted to see the End of Time.
Greed guided them to their destruction,
In the City that climbed so high, yet fell so low,
They wanted to see the End of Time.

Once lustrous on a mountain top,
now reduced to rubble,
rotting in the ground.
In the City that climbed so high, yet fell so low.
They wanted to see the End of Time.

It sparkled in gold,
but everything turned to ash,
as they fulfilled their dreams,
In the City that climbed so high, yet fell so low.
They wanted to see the End of Time.

Full of avarice,
they wanted it all,
It was never enough.
In the City that climbed so high, yet fell so low.
They wanted to see the End of Time.

Blood boiled in the burning streets,
as the walls crumbled,
the defences were a trap.
In the City that climbed so high, yet fell so low.
They wanted to see the End of Time.

They died by fire, as the flames consumed.
Their Spirits are condemned
to relive their doom.
In the City that climbed so high, yet fell so low.
They wanted to see the End of Time.

Their ultimate tragedy will echo
through the dimensions,
their fate will be pronounced.
In the City that climbed so high, yet fell so low.
They wanted to see the End of Time.

-History of Haunted Cities, pg 234
-Terochus Arginos
Head Master of the Itosian School of Necromancy
-Dark Tales of Fantasy:
A Contract for Gold: The Cataclysm of Medhebah

Dark Tales of Fantasy: 'To Rule by Right'

Runes glowed around the sides of the alter that were unseen a moment before. Prince Coel Ahern watched in astonishment. "Magic, my Prince," Othion Tacur explained. "is the energy that courses through everything. It is the spark of life at the moment of creation. Magic is the force that binds everything together, from the largest star to the smallest blade of grass.

It is what protects us from Thebel's intense light and is the flash of electricity within the clouds. Magic  is the Hyaloid Veil that separates everything and is the Great Attraction that draws everything to itself. It is everywhere and in everything, the very space between all things. It is what makes our hearts beat. Magic is the greatest power there is and dominates all others. If someone learns to manipulate magic, they can harness infinite strength."

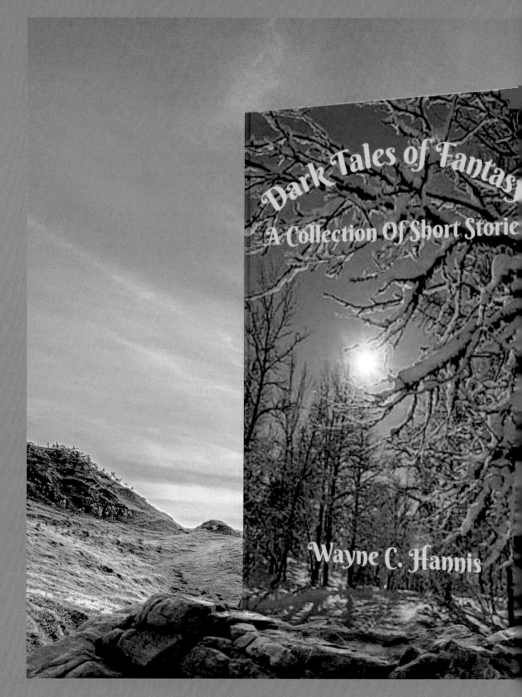

Dark Tales of Fantasy

In the end,
when Evil Things happen to
Good People,
there never is a happy
ending.

Five stories (novellas) of classic fantasy with a touch of horror from debut author Wayne C. Hannis.

Including: To Rule by Right
True Love Lost Forever
A Man Caught in Time
The Sword Cuts Deep
A Contract for Gold: The Cataclysm of Medhebah

www.waynehannis.ca

6. Other Poets
He who is Wise- listens!

"I saw old Autumn in the misty morn stand
shadowless like silence, listening to silence."
Thomas Hood
1799 - 1845

"Trees are the Earth's endless effort to
speak to the listening Heavens."
Rabindranath Tagore
1861 - 1941

"The Word 'listen' contains the same letters
as the Word 'silent'."
Alfred Brendel
American pianist-poet-author

"Listening is a magnetic and strange thing, a creative force. The friends who listen to us are the ones we move towards. When we are listened to, it creates us, makes us unfold and expand.
-Karl A. Menninger
1893 - 1990

"I cannot think that we are useless, or The Creator would not have created us. There is one Creator looking down on us all. We are all the Children of the One Creator. The Sun, the Darkness, the Winds are all listening to what we have to say."
Geronimo
1829 - 1909

What the Chimney Sang

By Brett Harte (Francis)
1836 - 1902

Over the chimney the night-wind sang, and
chanted a melody no one knew; and the Woman
stopped, as her babe she tossed, and thought of
the one she had long since lost, and said, as her
teardrops back she forced, 'I hate the wind in
the chimney'.

Over the chimney the night-wind sang and
chanted a melody no one knew; and the
Children said, as the closer they drew, 'Tis some
witch that is cleaving the black night through,
Tis a fairy trumpet that just then blew, and we
fear the wind in the chimney'.

Over the chimney the night-wind sang, and chanted a melody no one know; and the Man, as he sat on his hearth below, said to himself, 'It will surely snow, and fuel is dear and wages low, and I'll stop the leak in the chimney'.

Over the chimney the night-wind sang, and chanted a melody no on knew; But the Poet listened and smiled, for he was Man and Woman and Child, all three, and said, 'It is God's own harmony, this wind we hear'.

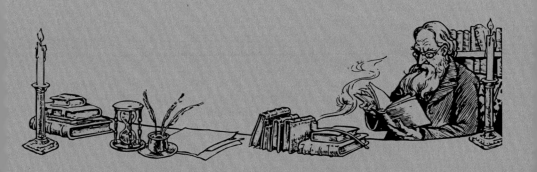

The Four ages of Man
By William Butler Yeats
1865 - 1939

He with body waged a fight,
But body won; it walks upright.
Then he struggled
with the heart;
Innocence and peace depart.
Then he struggled
with the mind;
His proud heart he left behind.
Now his wars on God begin;
At stroke of midnight God shall win.

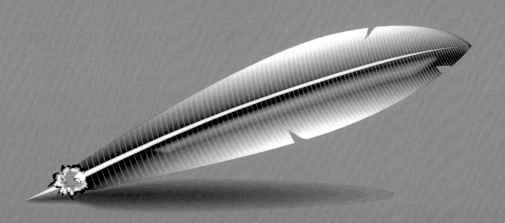

November 1836

By William Wordsworth
1770 - 1850

Even so for me a Vision sanctified
The sway of Death;
long ere mine eyes had seen
Thy countenance,
the still rapture of thy mien
When thou, dear Sister!
wert become Death's Bride:
No trace of pain or languor could abide
That change: age on thy brow
was smoothed thy cold
Wan cheek at once was privileged
to unfold
A loveliness to living youth denied.
Oh! if within me hope should e'er decline.
The lamp of faith, lost Friend!
too faintly burn;
Then may that heaven-revealing smile
of thine,
The bright assurance, visibly return:
And let my spirit in the power divine
Rejoice, as, through that power, it ceased
to mourn.

The Worker and the Work

By Ella Wheeler Wilcox
1850 - 1919

In what I do I note the marring flaw,
The imperfections of the work I see;
Nor am I one who rather
DO than BE,
Since its reversal is Creation's law.

Nay, since there lies a better
and a worse,
A lesser and a larger, in men's view,
I would be better than the thing I do,
As God is greater than His universe.

He shaped Himself
before He shaped one world:
A million eons, toiling day and night,
Before the planets into space
were hurled.

And when Creation's
early work was done,
What crude beginnings
out of chaos came:
A formless nebula, a wavering flame,
An errant comet, a voracious Sun.

And, still unable to perfect His plan,
What awful creatures at His touch
found birth:
Those protoplasmic monsters
of the earth,
That owned the world
before He fashioned Man.

And now, behold
the poor unfinished state
Of this, His latest masterpiece!
Then why,
Seeing the flaws in my own work. should
I
Be troubled that no voice proclaims it
great?

Before me lie
the cycling rounds of years;
With this small earth will die
the thing I do:
The thing I am,
goes journeying onward through
A million lives, upon a million spheres.

My work I build, as best I can and may,
Knowing all mortal effort ends in dust.
I build myself, not as I may, but must,
Knowing, or good, or ill,
that self must stay.

Along the ages, out, and on, afar,
Its journey leads,
and must perforce be made.
Likewise its choice, with things of shame
and shade,
Or up the path of light,
from star to star.

When all these solar systems
shall disperse,
Perchance this labour,
and this self-control,
May find reward;
and my completed soul
Will fling in space, a little universe.

The Things We Dare Not Tell
By Henry Lawson
1867 - 1922

The fields are fair in autumn yet, and the
sun's still shining there,
But we bow our heads and we brood and we
fret, because of the masks we wear;
Or we nod and smile the social while, and
we say we're doing well,
But we break our hearts, oh, we break
our hearts! for the things we must not
tell.

There's the old love wronged ere the new
was won, there's the light of long ago;
There's the cruel lie that we suffer for,
and the public must not know.
So we go through life with a ghastly
mask, and we're doing fairly well,
While they break our hearts, oh, they kill
our hearts! do the things we must not
tell.

We see but pride in a selfish breast, while
a heart is breaking there;
Oh, the World would be such a kindly
world if all men's hearts lay bare!
We live and share the living lie, we are
doing very well,
While they eat our hearts as the years go
by, do the things we dare not tell.

We bow us down to a dusty shrine, or a
temple in the East,
or we stand and drink to the world-old
creed, with the coffins at the feast;
We fight it down, and we live it down, or
we bear it bravely well,
But the best men die of a broken heart
for the things they cannot tell.

A Man Doesn't Have Time In His Life

By Yehuda Amichai
1924 - 2000

A man doesn't have time in his life
to have time for everything.
He doesn't have seasons enough to have
a season for every purpose.
Ecclesiastes was wrong about that.

A man needs to love and to hate at the
same moment,
to laugh and cry with the same eyes,
with the same hands to throw stones
and to gather them,
to make love in war and war in love.
And to hate and forgive and remember
and forget,
to arrange and confuse, to eat and to
digest what history takes years
and years to do.

A man doesn't have time.
When he loses he seeks, when he finds
he forgets, when he forgets he loves,
when he loves he begins to forget.

And his Soul is seasoned,
his soul is very professional.
Only his body remains forever
an amateur.
It tries and it misses, gets muddled,
doesn't learn a thing,
drunk and blind in its pleasures
and its pains.

He will die as figs die in autumn,
Shriveled and full of himself and sweet,
the leaves growing dry on the ground,
the bare branches pointing to the
place
where there's time for everything.

A Lament For The Wissahickon (Valley)
By Frances Anne Kemble
1809 - 1893

The Waterfall is calling me
With its merry gleesome flow,
And the green boughs
are beckoning me,
To where the wild flowers grow.

I may not go, I may not go,
To where the sunny waters flow,
To where the wild wood flowers
blow;
I must stay here
In prison drear,
Oh, heavy life, wear on, wear on,
Would God that thou wert done!

The busy mill-wheel round
and round
Goes turning, with its reckless
sound,
And o'er the dam the waters flow
Into the foaming stream below,
And deep and dark away they glide,
To meet the broad, bright river's
tide;
And all the way
They murmuring say:
"Oh, child!
why art thou far away?
Come back into the sun,
and stray
Upon our mossy side!"

I may not go, I may not go,
To where the gold-green waters run,
All shining in the summer sun,
And leap from off the dam below
Into a whirl of boiling snow,
Laughing and shouting as they go;
I must stay here
In prison drear,
Oh, heavy life, wear on, wear on,
Would God that thou wert done!

The soft spring wind goes passing by,
Into the forests wide and cool;
The clouds go trooping through the
sky,
To look down on some glassy pool;
The sunshine makes the world
rejoice,
Call me away,
With them to stay,
The blessed, livelong summer's day.

I may not go, I may not go,
Where the sweet breathing spring
winds blow,
Nor where the silver clouds go by,
Nor where the sunshine, warm and
bright,
Comes down like a still shower of
light;
I must stay here
In prison drear,
Oh, heavy life, wear on, wear on,
Would God that thou wert done!

O, that I were a thing with wings!
A bird, that in a May-hedge sings!
A lonely heather bell that swings
Upon some wild hill-side;
Or even a silly, senseless stone,
With dark, green, starry moss o'er
grown,
Round which the waters glide.

The Road not Taken

By Robert Frost
1874 - 1963

Two roads diverged in a yellow wood,
And sorry I could not travel both
And be one traveler, long I stood
And looked down one
as far as I could
To where it bent in the undergrowth.

Then took the other, as just as fair,
And having perhaps
the better claim,
Because it was grassy
and wanted wear;
Though as for that the passing there
Had worn them really
about the same.

And both that morning equally lay
In leaves no step had trodden black,
Oh, I kept the first for another day!
Yet knowing how way
leads on to way,
I doubted
if I should ever come back.

I shall be telling this with a sigh
Somewhere ages and ages hence:
Two roads diverged in a wood,
and I-
I took the one less traveled by,
And that has made all the difference.

Dawendine
By Emily Pauline Johnson
1861-1913

There's a spirit on the river,
there's a ghost upon the shore,
They are chanting, they are singing
through the starlight evermore,
As they steal amid the silence,
And the shadows of the shore.

You can hear them when the Northern
candles light the Northern sky,
Those pale, uncertain candle flames,
that shiver, dart and die,
Those dead men's icy finger tips,
Athwart the Northern sky.

You can hear the ringing war-cry of a
long-forgotten brave
Echo through the midnight forest, echo
o'er the midnight wave,
And the Northern lanterns tremble
At the war-cry of that brave.

And you hear a voice responding,
but in soft and tender song;
It is the Dawendine's spirit singing,
singing all night long;
And the whisper of the night wind
Bears afar her Spirit song.

And the wailing pine trees murmur with their
voice attuned to hers,
Murmur when they 'rouse from slumber as the
night wind through them stirs;
And you listen to their legend,
And their voices blend with hers.

There was feud and there was bloodshed near
the river by the hill;
And Dawendine listened,
while her very heart stood still:
Would her kinsman or her lover
Be the victim by the hill?

Who would be the great unconquered? who
come boasting how he dealt
Death? and show his rival's scalplock fresh
and bleeding at his belt.
Who would say, "O Dawendine!
Look upon death I dealt?"

And she listens, listens -
till a war-cry rends the night,
Cry of her victorious lover,
monarch he of all the height,
And his triumph wakes the horrors,
Kills the silence of the night.

Heart of her! it throbs so madly,
then lies freezing in her breast,
For the icy hand of death has chilled the
brother she loved best;
And her lover dealt the death-blow;
And her heart dies in her breast.

And she hears her mother saying,
"Take thy belt of wampum white;
Go unto yon evil savage
while he glories on the height;
Sing and sue for peace between us:
At his feet lay wampum white.

"Lest thy kinsmen all may perish,
all thy brothers and thy sire
Fall before his mighty hatred
as the forest falls to fire;
Take thy wampun pale and peaceful,
Save they brothers, save thy sire."

And the girl arises softly,
softly slips toward the shore;
Loves she well the murdered brother, loves
his hated foeman more,
Loves, and longs to give the wampum;
And she meets him on the shore.

"Peace," she sings, "O mighty victor, Peace! I
bring thee wampum white.
Sheathe thy knife whose blade has tasted my
young kinsmen's blood to-night
Ere it drink to slake its thirsting,
I have brought thee wampum white."

Answers he, "O Dawendine!
I will let thy kinsmen be,
I accept thy belt of wampum;
but my hate demands for me
That they give their fairest treasure,
Ere I let thy kinsmen be.

"Dawendine, for thy singing, for thy suing, war
shall cease;
For thy name, which speaks of dawning, Thou
shalt be the dawn of peace;
For thin eyes whose purple shadows tell
of dawn,
My hate shall cease.

"Dawendine, Child of Dawning,
hateful are thy kin to me;
Red my fingers with their heart blood,
but my heart is red for thee:
Dawendine, Child of Dawning,
Wilt thou fail or follow me?"

And her kinsmen still are waiting her
returning from the night,
Waiting, waiting for her coming with her belt
of wampum white;
But forgetting all, she follows,
Where he leads through day or night.

There's a spirit on the river,
there's a ghost upon the shore,
And they sing of love and loving
through the starlight evermore,
As they steal amid the silence,
And the shadows of the shore.

The Pine Tree

1st Pubished 1887 in 'Canada and
other poems'
Thomas Frederick Young
died 1940

The wind last night was wild and strong,
It shriek'd, it whistl'd and it rowr'd,
And went with whirl and swoop along,
'Mid falling trees and crashing board.

The timbers creak'd, the rafters sway'd,
And e'en some roofs, upheav'd and torn,
Came crashing to the earth, and laid
Before the view, upon the morn.

The air seem'd like some monstrous thing,
By its uncurbed passion held;
Like dreadful dragon on the wing,
So horribly it scream'd and yell'd.

Now venting a triumphant shout,
And ever and anon a groan,
Like fiend from prison lately out,
Or like unhappy chain'd one's moan.

There was a lofty pine I knew;
Each morn and eve I passed it by;
To such a lofty height it grew,
It caught at once each passing eye.

It stood alone, and proudly stood,
With straight, and clean, and lofty stem;
As though it scorn'd to live with them.

Full many a winter's snow had whirl'd
About its base, and settl'd there,
And many an autumn mist had curl'd
About its head, so high in air.

Full many a blast had spent, in vain,
Its force, for, ever like a rock,
It stood each persevering strain,
And long defied the tempest's shock.

But yesternight it crashing fell,
And now, this morn, I see it lie.
I knew the brave old tree so well,
A tear almost bedims my eye.

But brave old trees, like brave old men,
Must feel at last the fatal stroke,
That dashest them to earth again,
Tho' lofty pine, or mighty oak.

I'll miss, old tree, thy lofty stem
Outlin'd against the distant sky,
But 'tis no gain to fret for them—
For men, or trees, that fall and die.

A Ghost of Yesterday
By Madison Julius Cawein
1865 - 1914

There is a house beside a way,
Where dwells a ghost of Yesterday:
The old face of a beauty, faded,
Looks from the garden: and the shaded
Long walks of locust-trees, that seem
Forevermore to sigh and dream,
Keep whispering low a word that's true,
Of shapes that haunt its avenue,
Clad as in days of belle and beau,
Who come and go
Around its ancient portico.

At first, in stock and beaver-hat,
With flitting of the moth and bat,
An old man, leaning on a cane,
Comes slowly down the locust lane;
Looks at the house; then, groping, goes
Into the garden where the rose
Still keeps sweet tryst with moth and mo
And, humming to himself a tune,
"Lorena" or "Ben Bolt" we'll say,
Waits, bent and gray,
For some fair ghost of Yesterday.

The Yesterday that hold his all
More real to him than is the wall
Of mossy stone near which he stands,
Still reaching out for her his hands
For her, the girl, who waits him there,
A lace-gowned phantom, dark of hair,
Whose loveliness still keeps those walks,
And with whose Memory he talks;
Upon his heart her happy head,
So it is said,
The girl, now half a century dead.

Builders of Ruins

By Alice Christiana Thompson Meynell
1887 - 1922

We build with strength the deep tower-wall
That shall be shattered thus and thus.
And fair and great are court and hall,
But how fair- this is not for us,
Who know the lack that lurks in all.

We know, we know how all too bright
The hues are that our painting wears,
And how the marble gleams too white;
We speak in unknown tongues, the years
Interpret everything aright,

And crown with weeds our pride of towers,
And warm our marble through with sun,
And break our pavements through with flowers,
With an Amen when all is done,
Knowing these perfect things of ours.

O days, we ponder, left alone,
Like children in their lonely hour,
And in our secrets keep your own,
As seeds the colour of the flower.
To-day they are not all unknown,

The stars that 'twixt the rise and fall,
Like relic-seers, shall one by one
Stand musing o'er our empty hall;
And setting moons shall brood upon
The frescoes of our inward wall.

And when some midsummer shall be,
Hither will come some little one
(Dusty with bloom of flowers is he),
Sit on a ruin in the late long sun,
And think, one foot upon his knee.

And where they wrought, these lives of ours,
So many-worded, many-souled,
A North-west wind will take the towers,
And dark with colour, sunny and cold,
Will range alone among the flowers.

And here or there, at our desire,
The little clamorous owl shall sit
Through her still time; and we aspire
To make a law (and know not it)
Unto the life of a wild briar.

Our purpose is distinct and dear,
Though from our open eyes 'tis hidden.
Thou, Time-to-come, shalt make it clear,
Undoing our work; we are children chidden
With pity and smiles of many a year.

Who shall allot the praise, and guess
What part is yours and what is ours?
O years that certainly will bless
Our flowers with fruits, our seeds with flowers,
With ruin all our perfectness.

Be patient, Time, of our delays,
Too happy hopes, and wasted fears,
Our faithful ways, our wilful ways,
Solace our labours, O our seers
The seasons, and our bards the days;

And make our pause and silence brim
With the shrill children's play, and sweets
Of those pathetic flowers and dim,
Of those eternal flowers my Keats
Dying felt growing over him.

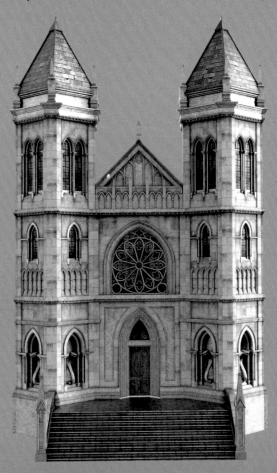

A Dream within a Dream
Edger Allen Poe
1809 - 1849

Take this kiss upon the brow!
And, in parting from you now,
Thus much let me avow —
You are not wrong, who deem
That my days have been a dream;
Yet if hope has flown away
In a night, or in a day,
In a vision, or in none,
Is it therefore the less gone?
All that we see or seem
Is but a dream within a dream.

I stand amid the roar
Of a surf-tormented shore,
And I hold within my hand
Grains of the golden sand —
How few! yet how they creep
Through my fingers to the deep,
While I weep — while I weep!
O God! Can I not grasp
Them with a tighter clasp?
O God! can I not save
One from the pitiless wave?
Is all that we see or seem
But a dream within a dream?

Mahabharata

Selected Poems

Sanskrit epic of Ancient India,
Longest Poem ever writen.
Detailing the events between
the 9th & 8th Centuries.
Author: Krishna Dvaipayana (Vyasa) c.400BCE.
Translated by: William Buck

"Tell me a story."
Now the wonderful world is born,
In an instant it dies,
In a breath it is renewed.

What is this life flowing?
In our bodies like fire?
What is it?
Life is like hot iron,
Ready to pour.
Choose the mould,
And life will burn it.

It is better to blaze up,
even for a moment,
than to smoulder forever with desire.
From the slowness of our eye,
And the quickness of God's hand-
We believe in the World.

Listen- I will speak of honour among men,
and of true love long remembered,
as in the stories of Kings and Demons that are
told to children by old people.

As Lord Brahma sleeps,
he hears something lost mentioned in his
dreams of life,
and he remembers
and it appears again here among us as it was
long ago.

Earth is strewn over with bright weapons and red with blood.
She resembles a dark dancing girl dressed in crimson, fallen confused with wine,
her golden bells and silver ornaments all deranged.

But it is illusion. It is done in play.
Who has been slain?
Who has done murder here?

Wealth and power pass like a dream,
Beauty fades like a flower,
Long life is gone like a wave.
I am not a clown, I am not a Beautiful Woman,
What have I to do in the palaces of kings?

The long grass bends,
Oh, the long grass in the dry wind,
Oh, the wind sharp as arrows,
Cut by the sword, the long grass swords.

I am the sweet wind,
The god's messenger,
And I am Desire:
Away with the cares of the world!

The One muttering the Veda to destroy me:
I over reach him;
I become the Soul of Virtue;
I become his own voice.

Then one trying to wear me down by
patience:
To him I am Strength of Truth;
He will never notice it is I.
And the Man with heavy books who would
kill me for Salvation:
I frolic and laugh in his face!

Away, away...
Away with the cares of the World...

Whoever reads of this battle between the Kurus that is like a sacrifice with sugar grains and butter, and whoever hears of it ever without malice, the Fire Lord and the Wind will be pleased with him, and the Moon and the Sun forever, Vyasa has written this song that all men may have no sickness and have great wealth, and victory, and food, and every bliss in heaven, and to him no man is high and none is low. Again, all men are kings to him. God is eternal, and because it is God who is praised here, it is for his that such merit is gained by hearing of the olden time as equals that from the giving of cows, by day and by night for one year, with their calves, to those who deserve.

The words of Vyasa can never be untrue.

New Fantasy Novel in the works from Wayne C. Hannis

'Giants will Come' (tentative title)

The Beginning of All Things

Before the creation of all things, long before anything came into being, there was the Aether. The Aether permeated throughout when there was nothing. Only the Aether existed before the beginning.

Out of the Aether, The Source of Consciousness and All Things emerged. He subsisted everywhere, like the Aether He originated from.

After a time, The Source became lonely. Above all else, He hoped for a Companion to be His equal in all things, and hope became part of the Aether.

Out of the Aether came His companion, as He hoped. She embodied His equal in all things, but She remained opposite, and He loved Her.

She named Him, 'Suneidesis', and He named Her, 'Dianoia'.

From Suneidesis and Dianoia the Four Elemental Spirits, their children, arose. The Salamander, The Undine, The Gnome and The Slyph came to be. The Four Elements of the Aether- Fire, Water, Earth and Air, that which make up all things, resulted from the Four Elemental Spirits.

Suneidesis designed a garden for Dianoia to tend, and She loved the garden He created. Dianoia tended it diligently, while the garden bloomed. The Four Elemental Spirits, their children, lived within the garden and helped it thrive.

The garden developed, and in the garden The One Tree sprang up, which became Dianoia's favourite. Dianoia gave everything to The One Tree, and She grew tall as Dianoia sang to Her. Life flourished under Her wide branches.

Soon The One Tree realized who and what She was, while She cast Her seeds abroad onto the fertile earth that came from the Four Elements of the Aether.

This comprised The Time of the Beginning. Only what The One Tree has enabled the Elves to remember in their many lifetimes, and the Dwarves to write in books, has transmitted through the Aeons in myth.

The First Aeon: The Age of Contentment

The One Tree imagined what could be, like Suneidesis had done before Her. The Elves and Dwarves composed the first of The One Tree's children. She cared for them as they cared for Her. From the deep roots of The One Tree and the fertile earth that came from the Four Elements of the Aether, the Dwarves existed first. They remained in their caverns to care for the roots of The One Tree, where their population grew as they constructed immaculate cities deep underground. Suneidesis revealed Himself to the Dwarves, and they revered Him.

As The One Tree's sharp needles settled onto the earth that comes from the Four Elements of the Aether, the Elves came into being. The Elves loved The One Tree and vowed to be Her guardians for all time. They dwelt close to Her, as She sheltered them under Her branches.

Dianoia, noticing the devotion of the Elves and the Dwarves to The One Tree, blessed them with long life. The Elves became special to Her, and She allowed them to know Her.

During the Age of Contentment all the animals, birds, reptiles, and insects, with every marvellous creature that ever was and ever will be, came from The One Tree's imagination and the rich earth that came from the Four Elements of the Aether. They multiplied and adapted throughout Her creation.

The One Tree grew as the First Aeon ended.

The Second Aeon: Time of the Titans

The Titans, personified from stone, were the first to come into being during the Second Age, and they became arrogant as they constructed lofty towers that reached the Baldachin. They were cruel and violent, destroying the earth that came from the Four Elements of the Aether and caused harm to The One Tree. They selfishly took from Her whatever they desired, and The One Tree suffered.

The Elemental Spirits created their children during the Second Aeon- the Salamander, the Undine, the Slyph, and the Gnome dwelt apart from the Titans, protected by The One Tree. The Wylde Creatures developed their Elemental magic, and dragons soared in the sky for the first time.

"The Sprites of fiery Termagants in Flame mount up and take a Salamander's name.

Soft yielding minds to water glide away and sip with Nymphs, their elemental tea.

The graver prude sinks downward to a Gnome, in search of mischief still on Earth to roam.

The light coquettes in Sylphs aloft repair, and sport and flutter in the fields of Air."

-Alexander Pope, The Rape of the Lock, Canto 1

At the end of The Second Aeon The One Tree grew, as the Earth that comes from the Four Elements of the Aether moved and became new again. The tall towers of the Titans shook in their foundations. The Wylde Creatures came forth and caused horrible war upon the Titans. The salamanders melted their vast cities of stone, and they became the Spired Mountains of Anian Regnum that ascend from the water. The One Tree utterly destroyed the Titans at the end of The Second Aeon.

The Third Aeon: Time of the Giants

The Giants came into being at the beginning of The Third Aeon from the remnants of the Titans. They were as cruel and violent as their predecessors. The Giants also hurt The One Tree, as they destroyed the earth that came from the Four Elements of the Aether, while constructing their architecture on the cornerstones of the Titans.

Corrupted cities rose from the Giants, profaning The One Tree. They created dangerous items of magic with the potential to destroy Her, as they attempted to escape the Baldachin.

The One Tree couldn't tolerate their existence, so as the Third Aeon ended and The One Tree prepared to grow, the Giants readied themselves for the end. However, The One Tree could not utterly destroy the Giants like She did with the Titans, for Her Spirit could not bring them to extinction. The One Tree, instead, separated the Giants unto themselves away from the rest of Her creation.

So concluded the Third Aeon as The One Tree grew again, and She protected all other creatures.

The Fourth Aeon: The Time of 'The Children of Earth'

Out of the water came The Children of Earth, they called themselves Human because of the diversity of colour in their skin, and the shades of light that emanated from them. The One Tree loved them, but they did not know The One Tree, for She resolved not to reveal Herself to them. Only through the teachings of the Elves and manuscripts of the Dwarves were they to know The One Tree.

Berthed in the Fourth Aeon, the Goblinkind were born from the mire of the Giants. They've hated humans since the beginning, waging constant war against them to energize their magic. The Goblinkind are like the Giants in their ways, prone to destruction and violence. They construct vast towers of twisted architecture to reach the sky, as they attempt to escape The Baldachin.

The humans created their glorious architecture in harmony with The One Tree, of whom they did not know. Until the families of The God-Kings came forth to assume power a thousand years ago- humans thought they were the Giants of old. The God-Kings now rule with their hidden agendas and create their architecture for their own purposes.

From this point, I can not write of what has not yet happened. The Fourth Aeon will soon end- I feel it- as The One Tree prepares to grow again, and what judgment She may bring is still unknown.

-Dwarven Lore: The Book of Aeons-Theodore Groundspike, Grand Master Mage of Suneidesis

About the Author

Wayne C. Hannis lives in the fantastic realm of the sunny Shuswap Lake in British Columbia, Canada and has called it home since he was a child. While growing up he played along creeks and in ravines, climbed ancient spruce trees and swam in clear fresh-water lakes- surrounded by nature it's no wonder his life is steeped with imaginative magic. Growing up Wayne played Dungeons and Dragons, while reading authors like David Eddings, Terry Brooks and Piers Anthony, they instilled his love for fantasy at a young age.

For most of his life Wayne has thought there's something wrong with our world, and has struggled to understand it. He has always had a passion for history, and with his study of what we have been taught, Wayne has come to realize that the narrative we all have been told wasn't the way it truly was in the past (as well as most things we are taught), and has struggled to find the real history of Us. Join Wayne as he ventures down those proverbial Rabbit Wholes in search of lost kingdoms and perhaps figure out what life is all about.   www.waynehannis.ca